WORLD BANK TECHNICAL PAPER NO. 368
Finance, Private Sector, and Infrastructure Network

W0017570

Privatization and Restructuring in Central and Eastern Europe

Evidence and Policy Options

*Gerhard Pohl, Robert E. Anderson,
Stijin Claessens, and Simeon Djankov*

*The World Bank
Washington, D.C.*

Technical Papers are published to communicate the results of the Bank's work to the development community with the least possible delay. The typescript of this paper therefore has not been prepared in accordance with the procedures appropriate to formal printed texts, and the World Bank accepts no responsibility for errors. Some sources cited in this paper may be informal documents that are not readily available.

The findings, interpretations, and conclusions expressed in this paper are entirely those of the author(s) and should not be attributed in any manner to the World Bank, to its affiliated organizations, or to members of its Board of Executive Directors or the countries they represent. The World Bank does not guarantee the accuracy of the data included in this publication and accepts no responsibility whatsoever for any consequence of their use. The boundaries, colors, denominations, and other information shown on any map in this volume do not imply on the part of the World Bank Group any judgment on the legal status of any territory or the endorsement or acceptance of such boundaries.

ISSN: 0253-7494

Photo: World Bank / IFC

The authors work on the Private Sector and Finance Team in the Europe and Central Asia/Middle East and North Africa Technical Department of the World Bank. Gerhard Pohl is manager of the team, Robert E. Anderson is senior private sector development specialist, and Simeon Djankov is a consultant to the team. Stijn Claessens is principal economist in the Office of the Vice President, East Asia.

Library of Congress Cataloging-in-Publication Data

Privatization and restructuring in Central and Eastern Europe :
    evidence and policy options / Gerhard Pohl . . . [et al.].
        p.   cm. — (World Bank technical paper   ; no. 368)
    Includes bibliographical references (p.   ).
    ISBN 0-8213-3975-3
    1. Privatization—Europe, Eastern.   2. Structural adjustment
(Economic policy)—Europe, Eastern.   3. Europe, Eastern—Economic
policy—1989-   I. Pohl, Gerhard.   II. Series.
HD4140.7.P7525   1997   97-13342
338.947—dc21   CIP

Contents

Tables

Figures

Boxed text

Summary

The countries in Central and Eastern Europe must determine what policies will most encourage enterprise restructuring, which is essential for the transition to a normal market economy and for accession to the European Union. Restructuring involves shedding surplus labor, manufacturing higher quality products, finding new markets in Western countries, and spinning off social and unneeded assets.

In this paper, we analyze the financial and operating data (1992 to 1995) for more than 6,300 industrial firms in seven countries of the region: Bulgaria, Czech Republic, Hungary, Poland, Romania, Slovak Republic, and Slovenia. We compare the extent of restructuring across firms in these seven countries to determine which country's policies are most effective in encouraging restructuring. All firms were previously owned by the state and many still are. These firms account for 40 to 95 percent of the industrial employment in these countries.

In our analysis we examined the following measures of restructuring:

- Profitability
- Proportion of firms with a positive operating cash flow,
- Average operating cash flow as a percent of revenue,
- Growth in labor productivity,
- Growth in total factor productivity, and
- Growth in exports.

The results were consistent for all six measures.

We next used econometric analysis to identify the government policies that most encouraged firms to restructure. In this analysis, we used as the measure of restructuring the increase in total factor productivity (the increase in output relative to the increase in all inputs).

Although substantial progress towards profitability was made in five of the countries (Czech Republic, Hungary, Poland, Slovak Republic, and Slovenia), the firms are not as profitable as those in a developed market economy (in which typically 95 percent of the firms are profitable). In contrast, firms in Bulgaria and Romania showed little improvement in profitability over this period.

Privatization had a large impact on restructuring. On average, a firm that has been privatized for four years will increase productivity 3-5 times more than a similar firm that is still in state ownership.

We found little difference in productivity between privatized firms in countries that used mass privatization methods (Czech and Slovak Republics, Poland) and in the other countries, which, until recently, have used standard (case-by-case) methods. In other words, either method of privatization for the same period of time will (on average) show the same degree of restructuring.

Based on an econometric analysis of Czech firms, we found that firms with concentrated ownership have restructured more than firms with dispersed ownership. Firms with loans from and ownership ties to banks restructured even more. This suggests that banks may be able to better monitor the performance of managers and encourage restructuring if they are both owners and lenders to the firms.

There are two related policy questions concerning the role of banks in the restructuring of firms. The first question is whether governments should recapitalize the large banks (typically still state-owned) to compensate for their bad loans. The second question is whether banks should be encouraged to forgive (write-off) bad loans made to firms. Enterprise managers often argue that these two policies will allow them to restructure more easily.

Our econometric analysis examined first whether additional bank lending actually encourages restructuring. The results are mixed. In the early years of transition, additional bank lending in all countries except for Hungary was actually associated with a decline in subsequent productivity and profitability. This suggests that bank loans were not helping to restructure firms but were financing their losses. By 1995, however, banks in five out of the seven countries seemed to be making more sound lending

Privatization is __the__ key to restructuring.

Different privatization methods show similar results.

decisions and supporting restructuring. The exceptions were Bulgaria and Romania.

When we divided the sample into privatized and state-owned firms, it turned out that poor bank lending was associated with state-owned firms. In all countries banks make sound lending decisions for privatized firms, but continued to support ailing state firms.

Imprudent bank lending is mostly to state-owned firms

We next examined firms burdened by large loans from banks that they cannot currently repay. We found that high levels of indebtedness at the start of transition did not hinder restructuring. One reason is that such firms may be under greater pressure to restructure. Another related reason is that firms in the region seem to be ingenious at finding sources other than loans from banks to finance restructuring. These sources may include loans from new private banks, credits from foreign buyers, new equity, joint ventures, and, most importantly, the firm's own cash flow.

We also found that the amount of bad loans and thus the need to recapitalize the banks is declining in those countries with rapid restructuring. We estimated the ability of firms in our data set to repay their bank loans based on their operating cash flow.

We conclude that recapitalizing banks and encouraging them to forgive loans is unlikely to help firms restructure very much. In fact, poor bank lending practices may discourage restructuring and result in additional bad loans. A safer course of action is to recapitalize banks only at the time of their privatization and after a large share of enterprises are privatized. That way there is more certainty that new bank owners will improve the quality of lending, support restructuring, and avoid another increase in bad loans.

Acknowledgments

This paper was written by Robert E. Anderson, Simeon Djankov, and Gerhard Pohl, (World Bank, Europe and Central Asia and Middle East and North Africa Technical Department, Private Sector Development and Finance Group), and Stijn Claessens (World Bank, Office of the Regional Vice President, East Asia and Pacific). The opinions expressed are not necessarily those of the World Bank.

We would like to thank Ying Lin and Faten Hatab for the excellent research assistance and Kiril Gatev and Petko Shishkov in Bulgaria, Petr Kucera in the Czech Republic; Csaba Tancsoz and Mihaly Kopanyi in Hungary; Jan Macieja in Poland; Arabela Aprahamian in Romania; Eva Kostrecova and Agnesa Szucsova in the Slovak Republic; and Mojca Jancar and Romania Logar in Slovenia for help with the data and data definitions. Alan Gelb, Cheryl Gray, Iraj Hashi, Elena Kotova and various seminar participants at the World Bank, University of Michigan, the Czech Economic Association, and the European Bank for Reconstruction and Development provided useful comments.

For comments or further information, please contact: Tel: (202) 473-8272; Fax: (202) 477-8772; or e-mail: sdjankov @worldbank.org.

Introduction

Only through improvements in firm productivity and profitability will there be an increase in the overall standard of living in transition economies. One of the most important tasks in the transition to a market economy is the restructuring of formerly state-owned firms. This restructuring can be thought of as the initial transition from a *highly distorted* economy with many large loss-making firms to a *normal* market economy in which most firms are profitable.

Restructuring is also a precondition for accession to the European Union, which is an objective of many countries in Central and Eastern Europe. Firms in these countries must be able to compete with EU firms without the need for subsidies or excessive risk of bankruptcy and loss of employment.

Restructuring of firms is also closely linked to the health of the banking system. Operational restructuring of firms means that they can pay a larger share of their bank loans and thus limit the bad loans held by banks. This may lessen or even eliminate the need to recapitalize the state-owned banks through government-led programs. Healthy firms are a condition for a healthy financial system.

We have obtained data on the performance of industrial firms in seven countries of the region (Bulgaria, Czech Republic, Hungary, Poland, Romania, Slovak Republic, and Slovenia). These countries have adopted different policies to encourage restructuring; thus these data can suggest which policies have been the most successful. In this paper, we summarize and extend our recent research using data for 1992-1995,[1] and we update our earlier study that was based on similar data for 1992-1994.[2]

We analyze a number of important issues concerning restructuring. First, we define what restructuring means and give examples from interviews with 21 firms in the Slovak Republic. We then examine the change in firm profitability in these seven countries over the period 1992 to 1995. In addition to profitability, we use five other measures to determine which firms have restructured the most.

Next, we use econometric analysis to determine which government polices most encourage restructuring. These policies include speed of privatization, allocation of bank lending, and reduction of indebtedness. Finally, we examine the impact of bank lending on restructuring and the link between industrial restructuring and the health of the banking system.

What is industrial restructuring?

Restructuring is a complex process. Firms in all countries must continuously restructure to maintain profitability in the face of a changing economic environment, technological progress, and competition from other firms. This continual restructuring leads to higher productivity and economic growth.

In the early years of the transition to a market economy, firms in Central and Eastern Europe experienced severe demand and price shocks. Demand for their products from former socialist countries had declined, and they were forced to find new markets in Western countries with higher quality standards. Lowered trade barriers meant that they faced increased competition from imported products in their home markets. Finally, all countries experienced severe economic recession which led to lower domestic demand.

As a consequence of these shocks, many firms in the region became unprofitable. In some cases, their situation was so desperate that their sales revenue was not even adequate to pay their suppliers. They were classified as "value subtractors" because the market value of their production was less than the cost of the materials used. If these

Restructuring should be a continuous process.

---

[1] This includes Claessens et al. (1997a), Claessens et al. (1997b), Djankov and Pohl (1997), and Djankov and Hoekman (1997).

[2] The original study, Pohl et al. (1996) was based on firm-level data for Bulgaria, the Czech and Slovak Republics, Hungary, and Poland.

firms could not restructure their operations, they were unlikely to survive. Thus one fundamental measure of restructuring is whether firms are able to become profitable in the new economic environment.

In this paper, we make a distinction between operational restructuring and financial restructuring; operational restructuring is the primary objective.

Case studies

Restructuring involves many difficult changes in the operation of a firm. In order to gain an appreciation of the restructuring process, we interviewed the managers of 21 large, mostly troubled firms in the Slovak Republic operating in a wide variety of industries.[3]

The extent of restructuring in these firms was substantial. In the early years of transition, two-thirds had been large loss-makers and one-third were judged by management consulting firms to be nonviable. By the end of 1996, however, over two-thirds of them were profitable including one-half of the firms judged nonviable.

In the early years of transition, the sales revenues of these firms dropped; but by 1996, revenues (in constant dollars) had increased to the level of 1991. This suggests that managers had found new markets to take the place of those in former socialist countries. Labor productivity (measured by value added per worker) almost doubled from 1991 to 1996. Most of these firms had domestic owners (the majority of which were current or former managers) and received little foreign investment.

The examples from the Slovak Republic (Box 1) illustrate what a firm must do to restructure and thus return to profitability. The majority of managers and new owners were able to restructure their firms without large amounts of foreign investment, foreign management expertise, loans from state-owned banks, or government assistance. This is encouraging because outside assistance is unlikely to be available in large amounts for the thousands of former state-

Operational (not financial) restructuring is the primary objective.

> ## Box 1: Restructuring of firms in the Slovak Republic
>
> The managers of 21 large Slovak industrial firms (19 of which were private) were interviewed regarding the steps they took to restructure their firms. These steps include:
>
> 1. *Labor shedding* -- The number of workers was reduced by 46 percent from 1991 through 1996, which improved cash flow and made revenue available for investment.
>
> 2. *Wage stability* -- The average real wage for all firms was almost constant from 1991 to 1996 although there was considerable variability from firm to firm.
>
> 3. *Spinning off social and unneeded assets* -- Most firms transferred to local governments such assets as housing, recreational facilities, and cafeterias; and they sold assets no longer needed such as inventories and surplus equipment and machinery.
>
> 4. *New Western markets* -- In 1991, only 9 percent of output was sold to Western countries. By 1996, the output had increased to 47 percent. Generally this occurred because the Slovak firm had become a supplier or subcontractor to a Western firm rather than selling directly to final consumers.
>
> 5. *New products and quality improvement* -- In order to become a supplier to a Western firm, the Slovak firms had to change their product mix and improve quality standards. For example, two-thirds of the firms have obtained an ISO 9001 certificate for total quality assurance.

owned firms that must restructure. These firms must rely on their own skills and resources.

This is not to minimize the value of foreign investment and the advice from Western management experts. Foreign investors often bring skills that are in short supply in transition economies (e.g., marketing skills). Previous studies show, however, that foreign investors are usually attracted to firms with considerable market power that

---

[3] Djankov and Pohl (1997a).

Table 1: Characteristics of the database of industrial firms

Firm Characteristics	Bulgaria	Czech Republic	Hungary	Poland	Romania	Slovak Republic	Slovenia
No of Firms	828	706	1,044	1,066	1,092	905	727
No. of Employees, 1992	314,042	829,312	428,645	1,338,629	2,121,102	578,737	219,959
% of Total Industrial Employment	48	64	41	45	91	93	90
Employment in Each Sector (%)							
Food	12.0	5.4	11.2	8.7	8.4	13.7	10.4
Tobacco	0.8	1.5	2.6	1.1	1.6	0.8	1.9
Textiles	9.0	5.5	13.0	8.5	6.9	4.2	12.9
Apparel	5.1	2.3	3.7	1.9	1.1	3.4	5.8
Lumber	8.4	3.6	3.5	2.3	8.8	4.3	3.0
Furniture	2.8	1.2	2.8	2.0	5.5	1.6	3.2
Paper	3.1	1.5	1.6	1.4	1.5	1.9	1.7
Printing	0.7	3.3	0.9	0.4	5.1	2.9	1.1
Chemicals	6.7	2.3	8.0	7.9	8.8	7.6	8.0
Petroleum refining	3.8	2.6	4.4	3.2	6.7	1.0	1.0
Rubber	1.9	1.4	4.3	4.5	1.6	2.7	2.2
Leather	3.5	1.5	2.5	2.6	3.3	3.0	3.5
Stone, clay, glass	2.7	14.6	5.4	7.6	3.7	4.6	1.5
Primary metals	6.2	7.0	9.1	10.6	1.8	4.8	13.5
Fabricated metals	2.9	9.8	3.9	4.6	10.3	14.6	4.0
Non-electrical machinery	17.5	16.2	5.6	15.2	9.2	10.0	4.1
Electrical machinery	4.3	3.0	10.9	3.2	3.6	5.0	14.1
Transport equipment	0.8	12.6	3.7	11.6	9.0	8.8	2.4
Instruments	7.6	3.8	2.3	2.2	2.2	4.1	5.3
Miscellaneous	0.2	0.9	0.6	0.5	0.9	1.0	0.4

have already restructured.[4] It would be a mistake, then, for managers to rely on outside assistance that may not be available.[5]

---

[4] See Carlin et al. (1995) for a survey.

[5] A recent study, Djankov and Hoekman (1997b), documents the alternative paths through which Czech firms obtained access to foreign technology. In many cases, firms signed subcontracting agreements with (mostly) German and Austrian partners that later resulted in joint ventures. As part of the agreements, the foreign counterparts advised Czech managers on appropriate technologies and suppliers and frequently trained their workers in the use of new equipment.

Sample of firms

We measure the speed of restructuring using financial statements and operating information from a large sample of industrial firms in seven countries of the region (Table 1). These are all formerly or currently state-owned firms. In order to make the analysis comparable across countries, the sample excludes firms in the utility, banking, and agricultural sectors, and new private companies.

The number of firms in the sample for each country ranges from 700 to more than 1,000. These firms account for a large share of the employment in the industrial sector (ranging from 40 percent to more than 90 percent). The original sample for 1992 included almost all industrial firms. Firms were dropped from the original sample if data for some years were missing.[6]

The proportion of firms in each industrial subsector is similar from country to country. In most countries, there is a concentration of firms in food, textiles, chemicals, metals, machinery, and transport equipment. Some countries, however, have specialized in different subsectors, for example, the Czech Republic in the stone, clay, and glass subsector, Slovenia in electrical machinery, and Bulgaria in nonelectrical machinery.

The size of a typical firm in terms of employment differs somewhat from country to country with the largest firms found in Poland and Romania (Figure 1). This is not surprising since these countries have the largest economies. The average size of manufacturing firms in the region at the start of the transition was higher than in developed market economies, but this was due to the absence of small firms rather than the predominance of very large firms. Very large firms account for a larger share of manufacturing and employment in developed market economies than in the transition economies.

In making comparisons between countries, it is important that the accounting and financial data for firms be based on similar standards. We adjusted the data to reflect differences in standards both over time and

Figure 1: Median number of employees in sample firms by country (1992)

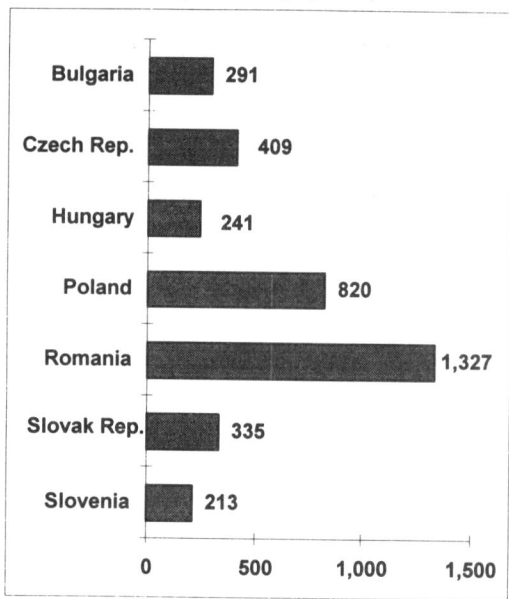

from country to country.[7] We also focused on measures of restructuring that incorporate the most reliable elements of the data. For example, we emphasize comparisons of operating cash flow (sales revenue less cost of inputs and wages). This measure does not into take account depreciation, debt service, and taxes, which are more likely to differ from country to country because of historical circumstances, differences in tax laws, or accounting standards.

Measures of profitability

The long term objective of restructuring is to improve the level of profitability of firms to a level similar to mature market economies in which almost all firms are profitable. Because a larger percentage of firms in the transition economies are unprofitable, it is useful to categorize the firms according to their degree of profitability or loss.

Polish firms in 1995 are used to illustrate this categorization (Table 2). The cate-

---

[6] This exclusion of firms from the sample for lack of data appeared to be random, and not to introduce a significant bias. The sample would be biased if the dropped firms were primarily the worst performers; for example, large loss makers that ceased to function or were liquidated. If this is important, it may overestimate the extent of aggregate restructuring in Bulgaria, Hungary, and Poland where (relatively) more firms were excluded from the sample.

---

[7] The main adjustments to the data were to reflect changes in the accounting for inventories (early in the period, increases in inventory was counted as a sale), and the fact that government subsidies were recorded as sales.

gories of profit or loss range from category A firms, which are profitable (after taxes) by international accounting standards, to category E firms, which are value subtractors. The categories are ranked based on the priority of paying expenses.

- *Category E* firms do not earn enough revenue to even cover the cost of material inputs much less pay any of the other operating costs. (Table 2 shows that 15 firms in this category have a negative operating margin.)

- *Category D* firms can pay their suppliers but cannot pay all of their workers. (Table 2 shows that 126 firms are in this category because they have a negative operating cash flow.)

- *Category C* firms can pay all of their workers and suppliers but cannot service all of their debts;, for example, they are behind in their interest payments to banks. (Table 2 shows that 130 firms are in this category because they have a negative cash flow after debt service.)

- *Category B* firms have enough revenue to cover all of their costs except for depreciation of the existing assets. This is not a payment to anyone else but reflects the fact that revenue is not adequate to maintain the level of productive capital. (Table 2 shows that 221 firms are in this category because they have a negative income before tax.)

- *Category A* firms can pay all of their costs, debt service, depreciation, taxes, and still have revenue left over. (Table 2 shows that 574 firms are in this category because they have a positive net income after tax.)

Comparing the number of firms in Category A for various countries (Table 3), the Czech Republic and Hungary had the highest percentage of profitable firms (74 percent and 70 percent respectively) and Romania and Bulgaria the lowest. In almost all countries, the profitability of firms has improved significantly (Table 3).

But there is also a great deal of variability in performance. Some firms show an improvement in their profitability while others show a decline. This variability is illustrated in a "transition matrix" for Polish firms (Table 4). Each row of numbers shows which firms in a particular category in 1992 moved to another category in 1995 or stayed

Firms were categorized according to degree of profit or loss.

Table 2: Profit/loss categories for Polish firms in 1995

	All Firms	Category A	Category B	Category C	Category D	Category E
Number of Firms	1,066	574	221	130	126	15
Employment: (1,000)	1,122	542	260	169	136	16
Employment %	100%	49%	23%	15%	12%	1%
Loans Outstanding %	100%	43%	26%	14%	15%	2%
Sales Revenue (mil. zloty)	93,655	45,761	28,459	11,244	7,116	1,074
(% of Revenue)						
Sales revenue	100.0%	100.0%	100.0%	100.0%	100.0%	100.0%
minus cost of materials and energy	80.6%	79.1%	80.7%	80.9%	84.4%	119.3%
= Operating margin	19.4%	20.9%	19.3%	19.1%	15.6%	**-19.3%**
minus wages and wage taxes	12.3%	9.3%	13.5%	16.6%	20.1%	8.5%
= Operating cash flow	7.1%	11.6%	5.8%	2.6%	**-4.5%**	-27.8%
minus net financial charges	3.2%	2.7%	2.9%	4.8%	4.6%	1.5%
= Cash flow after debt service	3.9%	8.9%	2.9%	**-2.2%**	-9.1%	-29.4%
minus depreciation	5.0%	4.2%	6.4%	4.9%	5.0%	1.9%
= Net income before tax	-1.0%	4.7%	**-3.5%**	-7.1%	-14.2%	-31.3%
minus income tax	1.3%	2.3%	0.3%	0.2%	0.3%	0.0%
= Net income after tax	-2.3%	**2.4%**	-3.9%	-7.3%	-14.4%	-31.3%

In 1995 50 percent of Polish firms were profitable.

Table 3: Industrial firms categorized by degree of profit or loss
(percentage of firms weighted by employment)

| | | | Unprofitable | | | | |
| | | Profitable | Cannot Cover Depreciation | Cannot Service all Debt | Cannot Pay all Wages | Cannot Pay all Suppliers | |
	Year	A	B	C	D	E	Total
Bulgaria	1995	45	13	17	22	4	100
(828 firms)	1994	43	11	29	13	4	100
	1993	22	18	23	32	5	100
	1992	28	10	31	27	4	100
Czech Republic	1995	73	19	6	1	1	100
(706 firms)	1994	71	20	6	3	0	100
	1993	63	25	10	2	0	100
	1992	60	11	15	13	1	100
Hungary	1995	70	14	6	9	1	100
(1,044 firms)	1994	67	11	9	11	2	100
	1993	67	9	8	12	4	100
	1992	59	9	12	14	6	100
Poland	1995	49	23	15	12	1	100
(1,066 firms)	1994	45	23	16	14	2	100
	1993	40	17	12	24	7	100
	1992	37	16	16	21	10	100
Romania	1995	24	16	9	40	11	100
(1,092 firms)	1994	23	13	11	40	14	100
	1993	24	16	8	42	10	100
	1992	30	7	9	41	12	100
Slovak Republic	1995	56	27	7	10	0	100
(905 firms)	1994	57	21	9	13	0	100
	1993	51	22	12	13	2	100
	1992	48	16	13	19	4	100
Slovenia	1995	64	17	9	8	2	100
(727 firms)	1994	67	14	13	6	0	100
	1993	67	13	15	5	0	100
	1992	65	13	17	5	0	100

In the Czech Republic 73 percent of firms are profitable.

In Romania, only 24 percent of firms are profitable.

in the same category. Both the number of firms and a percentage of the total is provided.

Using Category E firms (the worst performing firms) as an example, this matrix shows that 31 out of the 72 firms in this category in 1992 (43 percent) became profitable and moved into Category A by 1995. In contrast, 6 firms (8 percent) showed no improvement and remained Category E firms. At the opposite end, the profitability of some firms in Category A in 1992 declined over the period. Of the 498 profitable (Category A) firms in 1992, 333 firms (67 percent) remained profitable. The other 165 firms, however, became unprofitable and moved into the other four categories. Two of the profitable firms in 1992 actually moved into the worst loss-making category (Category E).[8]

Of the total 1,066 firms, 835 showed an improvement or stayed the same while 231 showed a decline. In comparing these matrices from one country to another, a matrix with the largest numbers at or below the diagonal (shaded area in Table 4) means that firms in that country are restructuring the most. In examining a similar matrix for firms in a developed market economy (United Kingdom), we found most loss-making firms improved or ceased operating.

Table 4: Transition matrix for Polish industrial firms (1992-95).

Number of Firms and Percent
by Profit and Loss Category

| | | | 1995 | | | |
		A	B	C	D	E	Sum
	A	333	94	38	31	2	498
		67%	19%	8%	6%	0%	100%
	B	50	41	22	10	0	123
		41%	33%	18%	8%	0%	100%
1992	C	39	27	33	27	1	127
		31%	21%	26%	21%	1%	100%
	D	121	47	33	39	6	246
		49%	19%	13%	16%	2%	100%
	E	31	12	4	19	6	72
		43%	17%	6%	26%	8%	100%

Total Number of Firms 1,066

Restructuring will be influenced by many random factors that cannot be controlled, including quality of management, location, initial conditions, sector, or just plain luck. The large variation suggests that although governments can put policies that encourage restructuring in place, not all firms will show equal improvement.

Measures of restructuring

In addition to profitability, we have used five other measures of restructuring:

Positive operating cash flow. A common problem in the early days of transition was that many firms were large loss-makers.

Thus the first measure of restructuring is the percentage of firms (weighted by employment) that have achieved at least a positive operating cash flow. This is defined to be sales revenue less cost of inputs and wages. In Table 3, this would include all firms in profit Categories A, B, and C. Conversely, this measure also indicates the proportion of firms in each country that are still large loss-makers. Once a firm has at least achieved this level of profitability, it can use its operating cash flow to service some of its debt and invest in modernization and growth.

- *Operating cash flow.* Although the first measure of restructuring indicates how many firms remain large loss-makers, it says nothing about the profitability of all firms. To measure this, we used the operating cash flow as a percentage of sales for all firms in the sample. Operating cash flow is again defined to be sales revenue less cost of inputs and wages.

- *Labor productivity.* One of the most difficult problems facing firms was the issue of surplus labor. As sales to their traditional markets declined, firms either had to find new markets or lay off surplus workers. To measure how firms coped with this problem, we measure the annual change in labor productivity over the period. Labor productivity is defined as value added (value of sales less cost of non-labor inputs measured in 1995 prices) divided by the man-hours of labor employed.

- *Total Factor Productivity.* This measures the success of a firm in increasing the productivity of all factors of production (labor, material inputs, and capital). In essence, an increase in total factor productivity occurs when output increases more than the inputs increase. Because multiple inputs are involved, however, this measurement has to be made using sophisticated statistical techniques. A companion paper explains the techniques used.[9]

---

[8] The percentages in Table 4 are not identical to those in Table 3 for Poland because the percentages in the earlier table are weighted by employment.

[9] The measurement of both labor productivity and total factor productivity are further described in Claessens et al. (1997b).

• *Growth in exports.* The firms in the region typically experienced a large decline in sales to their traditional markets in the former socialist countries. Thus an essential element of restructuring was to reorient sales to Western markets. This required firms to develop more sophisticated marketing techniques and to improve the quality of their products so that they could compete with Western companies producing the same products. The success of firms in re-orienting their sales to Western markets is measured by the increase in exports from 1992 to 1995.

For a given firm, the five restructuring measures tend to be highly correlated, but there are substantial differences in the pace of restructuring across firms in the region (Table 5). Czech firms rank at the top using most measures of restructuring. Hungarian, Polish, and Slovak firms are close behind. Firms in Bulgaria and Romania rank at the bottom. Analyzing differences in enterprise performance across these countries may shed light on which policies most favor restructuring.

Determinants of restructuring

Now we examine how the economic policies in those countries with the most restructuring differ from those countries with the least restructuring. Some of the economic policies that appear to be positively correlated with restructuring include:

• *Rapid privatization.* A firm would be either given away to all citizens (referred to as "coupon privatization" or "mass privatization") or go through management buy-outs.

• *Concentrated outside control over firms.* After the coupon privatization period investment funds controlled by the banks became the dominant owners of many firms in the Czech and Slovak Republics. In other countries such as Hungary, Poland, and Slovenia, many management/employee buy-outs took place. Finally, in Hungary and more recently in the Czech Republic and Poland, some firms were bought by strategic foreign investors.

• *Limiting wage increases.* Once a firm restructures and improves its cash flow, wage increases must be limited so that there is more revenue to finance new investment and further restructuring.

• *Financial discipline.* A firm is more likely to restructure if neither the government (through subsidies) nor the banks (through loans) finance the firm's losses. This financial discipline (sometimes referred to as a "hard budget constraint") forces firms to achieve at least a positive operating cash flow.

• *Maintaining debt obligations.* Firms may have a greater incentive to restructure and thus service their debts if banks do not forgive or reduce those debts.

Although they are important, the poli-

Table 5: Measures of restructuring for industrial firms

	Firms with Positive Operating Cash Flow (1995)	Average Operating Cash Flow as % of Revenue (1995)	Annual Growth in Labor Productivity (1992-95)	Annual Growth in Total Factor Productivity (1992-95)	Annual Growth in Exports in 1995 prices (1992-95)
Bulgaria	74%	1%	-2%	0%	14%
Czech Republic	98%	14%	7%	5%	22%
Hungary	90%	8%	3%	4%	11%
Poland	87%	7%	5%	5%	18%
Romania	49%	1%	-1%	-1%	6%
Slovak Republic	90%	12%	5%	5%	20%
Slovenia	90%	10%	3%	1%	8%

Table 6: Measures of privatization, 1995

| | EBRD (Rank) | OECD (Firms) | World Bank (Firms) | Industrial Firms | |
				(Firms)	(Output)
Bulgaria	2	15%		8%	7%
Czech Rep.	4	87%	90%	89%	93%
Hungary	4	82%	78%	67%	65%
Poland	3	55%	46%	61%	60%
Romania	3	20%		15%	12%
Slovak Rep.	3	74%		79%	83%
Slovenia	3	54%		41%	41%

Sources:
EBRD: *Infrastructure and Savings*, 1996, p. 11.
OECD: *Trends and Policies in Privatization*, 1996, p. 19.
World Bank: *From Plan to Market: World Development Report*, 1996, p. 53.
Industrial Firms: authors' estimates.

cies we describe here are not solely responsible for rapid restructuring.

Our database on large industrial firms in the region allows us to measure which factors most influence restructuring in all seven countries. To more accurately determine which economic policies allow for faster restructuring, we applied econometric analysis to the data (see Annex). This allows us to separate the various government policies from the other factors including size, sector, and initial level of productivity that also have an impact on restructuring. We summarize the results in the following sections.

Extent of privatization

Measuring the extent of privatization in a country is complicated, and cross-country comparisons are difficult. Does the measure of privatization just count the number of firms that have been privatized or does it take into account their size and importance? What firms are covered by the measure of privatization -- small firms, only medium and large firms, industrial firms, agricultural firms, utilities, or banks? When is a firm considered to be privatized -- when ownership is completely in private hands (100 percent), only a majority ownership (51 percent), or merely a significant minority ownership (say 25 percent)?

In Table 6 we include estimates of the extent of privatization in the seven countries. Because of the complexities in measuring the extent of privatization, the various measures are not always comparable across countries, but they all show similar rankings. We have also measured the extent of privatization for those firms in our data base. We define as "privatized" any firm that has more than 33 percent of its shares transferred to private investors (Table 6, last two columns). We measure the extent of privatization both by a simple count of the number of firms classified as privatized and a weighted average based on output to reflect differences in size.

On all measures the Czech Republic, Hungary, and the Slovak Republic were ahead of the other four countries. At the opposite end, Bulgaria was almost completely dominated by state-owned firms.

Impact of privatization

The impact of privatization on restructuring is very large. As shown in Table 7, labor productivity growth during 1992-95 averaged 7.2 percent per year, for privatized firms[10], but -0.3 percent for state-owned firms. In other words, privatization accounts

Privatization is the key to restructuring.

---

[10] Firms are taken as privatized if more than one third of their shares were in private hands by 1995.

Table 7: Labor productivity growth, 1992-95

(% p.a.)	Privatized firms[a]	State-owned firms
Bulgaria	12.4	-1.4
Czech Republic	8.6	-2.6
Hungary	6.0	3.2
Poland	7.5	1.4
Romania	1.0	-0.5
Slovak Republic	7.8	-4.1
Slovenia	7.2	1.8
Average	**7.2**	**-0.3**

[a] Firms privatized by 1995

Privatized firms show high rates of productivity growth.

for 70 to 90 percent of the labor productivity growth observed in countries with large privatization programs. The exception is Hungary, where state-owned firms achieve half the productivity gains of privatized firms. By contrast, in countries with insignificant privatization (e.g., Bulgaria and Romania), productivity in state-owned firms is deteriorating.

Similar results were obtained if total factor productivity (TFP) is taken as an indicator of restructuring. Figure 2 shows the cumulative increase in total factor productivity for privatized firms since the time of privatization and compares this with the TFP gains for state-owned firms in the sample. The econometric analysis in the

Figure 2: Change in total factor productivity

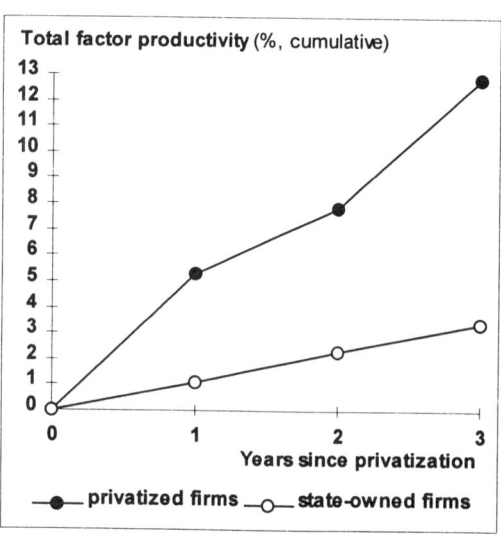

Different privatization methods show similar results.

Annex (Table A1) shows that privatization increases total labor productivity growth by about 4.5 percentage points per year over a period of at least four years (we do not have estimates for privatization effects beyond that period).

There is some evidence that managers carry out restructuring even in anticipation of privatization if the government's commitment to privatization is credible. For example, in the Polish mass privatization program, the 512 firms included in the program began to show rapid improvement in profitability in 1994 and 1995, compared to other state-owned firms, even though they were not formally privatized until November 1995. One explanation for this is that managers improve their performance when they expect to be held accountable by new owners and want to prove their ability as managers before privatization. Similarly, large privatization programs appear to have a positive impact on productivity in state-owned firms, probably due to similar anticipation and signaling effects.

Concentrated control over firms

Experts and government officials often argue, that the quality of privatization should not be sacrificed for the speed of privatization. This was the justification given for the slow pace of privatization in Bulgaria. Critics of mass privatization contend that fast privatization would result in widely dispersed ownership by small investors who do not have the skill, experience, capital, or incentive to restructure firms. They favor instead more conventional case-by-case privatization in which firms are sold to large investors (often foreign).

Until recently, Bulgaria, Hungary, Poland, and Slovenia have relied primarily on case-by-case privatization rather than mass privatization. However, Poland recently completed a limited mass privatization program, and Bulgaria is now implementing a program (see Box 2 for a description). Romania is revising and continuing its earlier program.

If the arguments in favor of case-by-case privatization were valid, the econometric analysis would show that case-by-case privatization of a firm has a bigger impact on their restructuring; i.e., the regression coefficients for the privatization variable would be smaller for mass privatized firms. Such a premise is not supported by the data. Mass privatization seems to result in the same speed of restructuring as other methods.

One explanation is that mass privatization did not result in dispersed ownership by many small investors. The structure of ownership became concentrated, often in the hands of large investment funds or successor holding companies. In the Czech Republic, for example, ownership concentration (measured by the share of the company owned by the five largest owners) was already high by 1993 and has increased substantially since then. Ownership concentration is even higher in the Slovak Republic (Table 8). In the Polish mass privatization scheme, the ownership by investment funds was high by design. In each of the mass privatized firms, 60 percent of all shares were given to the fifteen investment funds.

Table 8: Average combined ownership of five largest owners

Czech Republic -- 706 firms from first and second wave.	
1st Quarter 1993	50%
1st Quarter 1996	65%
Slovak Republic -- 623 firms from first wave.	
4th Quarter 1993	52%
4th Quarter 1995	73%

A complementary development in the Czech and Slovak Republics has been the transformation of many investment funds into holding companies. Instead of the funds having small minority stakes in many companies, these new holding companies have large majority stakes in just a few companies. The managers of the funds stated that they wanted to be the dominant majority shareholder in fewer firms.[11]

---

[11] Interviews with investment fund managers in the Czech Republic (March 1997) and Slovak Republic (December 1996).

Box 2: Mass Privatization in the Czech Republic, Poland, and Bulgaria

Mass privatization involves giving away ownership of state-owned firms to all citizens. The *Czech Republic* pioneered this method in 1991 and had privatized more than 1,600 firms by 1994 in two waves (the Slovak Republic only conducted the first wave). In some cases, a portion of a firm's shares were reserved for sale using conventional methods. A citizen was given (for a nominal charge) a coupon, which could be used to buy shares in a national auction in any firm included in the program.

Citizens could bid to buy shares with their coupons in any of the firms. Alternatively, they could decide to turn over their coupons to an investment fund and thus become part owner of a much larger and diversified portfolio. Almost anyone could establish a fund. About 70 percent of the coupons were turned over to 550 funds, which became the dominant owners of Czech firms.

In *Poland*, about 512 firms (representing only about 10 percent of all industry and construction in terms of sales) were recently mass privatized. In contrast to the Czech program, the government exercised more control over the ownership structure, which may have contributed to the fact that implementation took five years. The government distributed enterprise shares to 15 investment funds with a "lead fund" that had a controlling stake (33 percent) in each company. The rest was distributed to other funds, workers, and the government (25 percent) for later sale. The government held an international competition to select fund managers and specified the terms of their management contracts. Citizens were given a certificate entitling them to equal ownership in all 15 funds.

By mid-1997, *Bulgaria* will implement a program similar to the Czech program. Approximately 1,050 firms are included. About 80 percent of the citizens have turned their coupons over to approximately 100 investment funds. In contrast to the Czech program, the government is retaining a majority stake in many of the larger that are firms for sale using conventional methods. Thus, given the slow pace of conventional methods thus far and the current troubled economic situation, privatization is likely to remain slow.

Mass privatization encourages restructuring as much as other methods.

Ownership concentration accelerates restructuring.

Figure 3: Organization of a bank controlled fund

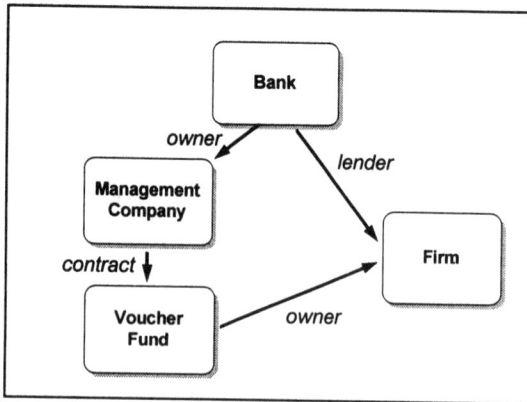

In 1996, there appears to have been further concentration of ownership in the Czech and Slovak Republics through mergers, acquisitions, and buyouts. This is sometimes called the "third wave" of privatization. In the Slovak Republic, for example, twelve of the former foreign trade companies have become holding companies with large ownership stakes in 146 industrial firms.[12]

A concentration of fund ownership parallel to the concentration of firm ownership allows this transformation of investment funds into holding companies. Large investors have bought the shares of the funds on the stock markets, accumulated controlling stakes, and then -- at a general meeting of fund shareholders -- approved a conversion of the fund into a holding company.

Many of these funds and holding companies in the Czech and Slovak Republics are controlled by large domestic banks (Figure 3). These banks own the management companies that established and now control the larger funds. There is concern that these banks both lend to firms and control the funds that own those firms. This dual role could present conflicts of interest that might impair restructuring.[13] For ex-

Many investment funds have become holding companies.

ample, the bank might require a firm to borrow from the bank at high interest rates to the detriment of other shareholders.

This dual role of banks as both (direct and indirect) owners and lenders is common in many countries notably, Germany and Japan, and does not seem to impair enterprise performance. In fact, such a bank would have a dual incentive both as an owner and a lender to ensure that the firm restructured and became profitable. The bank may also have better information about the operations of firms when it is both a lender and an owner, thus improving its ability to monitor the performance of firm management.

We find that both concentrated ownership and ownership by bank-controlled funds encouraged restructuring in the Czech Republic. In this analysis, the measure of restructuring is the value that the stock market places on the company relative to the book value of its assets (this ratio is called "Tobin's Q").[14] In other words, if investors believe that the company is restructuring and becoming profitable, they will bid up the prices of shares on the stock exchange. In our case, we are using investor's judgment about the extent of restructuring.

As shown in Figure 4, the stock market places a higher value on a company in the Czech Republic when ownership is more concentrated.[15] The value is increased further if ownership is in the hands of bank-controlled funds and increased further still if these banks are also the main lenders to the company. Although conflicts of interest may exist between the role of a bank as both owner and lender to a company, investors seem to believe that this is outweighed by the ability of the bank to monitor and control the managers and thus encourage more restructuring.

---

[12] Trend, (1996).

[13] This point is elaborated in Coffee (1996). Interviews with the five largest bank-sponsored investment funds by the authors (March 1997) showed that two of the funds maintained strong links with their bank-sponsor, while the other three acted independently.

[14] For a specific firm, Tobin's Q = [market valuation + total debt]/[net fixed assets + inventory]. Other measures, such as profitability show similar results.

[15] This relationship breaks down when a single investor has more than 50% of the shares of a firm. This is due to the weak minority shareholder protection in the Czech Republic. For earlier results see Claessens (1997).

Figure 4: Impact of ownership concentration and bank ownership on stock market valuation in the Czech Republic

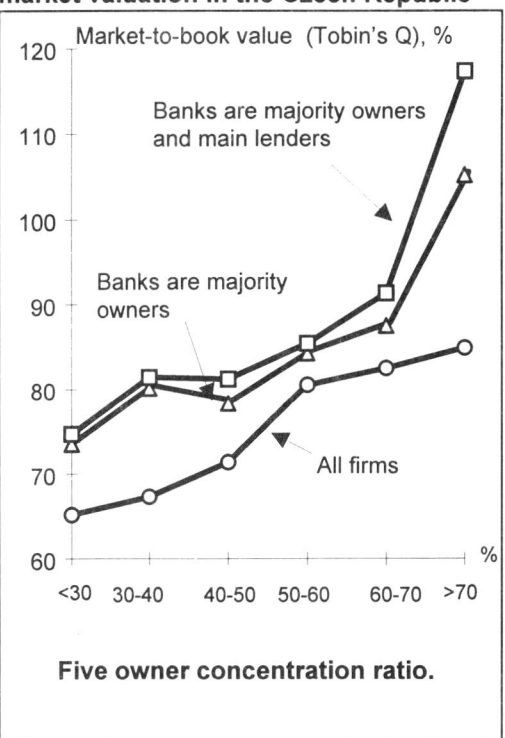

Five owner concentration ratio.

Another explanation for the relatively high level of restructuring in those countries that used mass privatization is that conventional case-by-case privatization did not result in higher quality owners that many had hoped for. Though detailed information on new owners is difficult to obtain, the level of foreign participation in case-by-case methods has been relatively low except for

Figure 5: Sources of privatization revenue -- end 1995

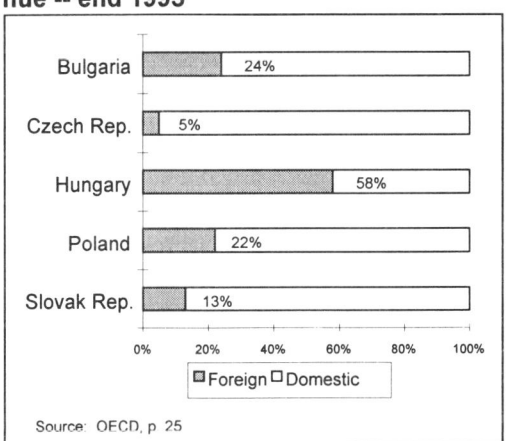

Hungary (see Figure 5). Instead, firms were more often sold to local domestic investors, in many cases, the managers and employees of the firms. For example, in Poland, about 2,500 small and medium state-owned firms were included in what was called "liquidation privatization." Most of these firms were purchased by managers and employees. There is considerable debate about whether management and employee-owned firms will perform better than mass privatized firms.

Role of banks

We use econometric analysis to measure the impact on restructuring of additional bank lending to firms. Theory and experience in the region show that additional lending can either encourage or discourage restructuring depending on the expertise, skills, and independence of the banks making the loans.

Additional lending will *encourage* restructuring if the banks are skilled at evaluating the future performance of the companies that wish to borrow money. The banks must be able to determine whether the firm managers will use the money to make profitable investments that help to restructure the firm. Only then can the banks be confident that the firm will generate the necessary revenue to repay the loans.

Additional lending will *discourage* restructuring if the banks lend money to firms that will only use it to cover current operating losses (for example, wages) instead of making productive investments. Not only are these bank loans not used for productive new investments, but they reduce the incentive for firm managers to restructure. Because the managers believe that bank loans will be available to cover current operating losses, they avoid the difficult and painful actions (such as laying-off workers) necessary to reduce operating losses.

In many countries of the region, the improved quality of bank lending now encourages restructuring for three reasons. First, in order to control inflation, central banks have reduced credit expansion so that banks have less to lend to loss-making firms. Second,

In early years, bank lending discouraged restructuring.

government officials have also learned that pressuring banks to lend for the purpose of covering firm losses and avoid worker lay-off cannot continue without jeopardizing macro-stability and quality of lending. Third, the banks themselves have improved their skills and can better evaluate the restructuring plans of firms before lending to them.

As a result, the state-owned banks in these countries have not increased their lending to firms. New private banks (often foreign-owned) have stepped in to fill the gap, and they are more likely to have the necessary skills to make good lending decisions. In the Slovak Republic, for example, about 80 percent of the recent increase in bank lending has come from new private banks. Outstanding loans by state-owned banks has shown little increase. Although this is sometimes viewed with concern -- especially by firms who have traditionally borrowed from these state-owned banks -- this is probably desirable until the state-owned banks can improve their lending skills and become more independent.

Our econometric analysis[16] supports this view of the evolution of bank lending. Early in the transition, bank lending did more harm than good. In 1993, for six of the seven countries we examined, an increase in bank lending to a firm was associated with either constant or declining productivity (Hungary was the exception). Two years later, however, the quality of bank lending had improved in three more countries (Czech and Slovak Republics, and Slovenia). Thus by 1995, in four out of the seven countries an increase in bank lending was associated with an increase (with a time lag) in a firm's total factor productivity. This suggests that firms used new bank loans to finance restructuring rather than merely cover current operating losses.

In 1995, the data suggests that banks in Bulgaria and Romania were still making poor lending decisions. This is no doubt a cause of the current economic crises in Bulgaria. Many firms are still loss-makers because they were not privatized and have

failed to restructure, and many banks are insolvent because they continued to make bad loans to these firms.

When we divided the sample into privatized and state-owned firms, the results show that poor bank lending is largely associated with state-owned firms. In all countries, banks made much better decisions in lending to private firms than to state owned firms. Lending to privatized firms was associated with an increase in productivity (with a time lag) already in 1992.

Wage restraint

Restructuring is likely to be encouraged if the work force does not initially absorb all of the productivity gains as higher wages. As noted above, firms must finance a large proportion of investment with retained earnings from current cash flow especially when the financial system is weak. If wages rise slower than labor productivity, more cash flow is available for investment. Put differently, a positive operating cash flow per worker only exists if labor productivity (value added per worker) exceeds wages. In the long run, the objective is to increase wages so that the workforce benefits from the restructuring of firms. In the short run, however, wage increases may have to be sacrificed to encourage faster restructuring.

Our analysis shows that the large productivity gains from privatization have been

Figure 6: Labor productivity and real wage growth for privatized and state-owned firms (% p.a.)

By 1995, bank lending in four out of seven countries encouraged restructuring.

In privatized firms, labor productivity growth leads wage growth.

---

16 Claessens et al. (1997b).

largely retained by firms to finance productivity-enhancing investments. For privatized firms, labor productivity growth has been faster than real wage growth in all countries (above the diagonal in Figure 6). In contrast, real wage growth in state-owned enterprises has exceeded labor productivity gains, eroding internally generated financing.

The rapid productivity growth in privatized firms has led to rapid growth in real wages. But since privatized firms maintained a larger margin between labor productivity and wage, they were also able to sustain high levels of investment per worker (Table 9).

Table 9: Investment per worker
(US$ annual average purchasing power parity, 1992-95)

(% p.a.)	Privatized firms	State-owned firms
Bulgaria	2,790	90
Czech Republic	3,290	470
Hungary	2,990	460
Poland	1,880	410
Romania	590	110
Slovak Republic	3,340	230
Slovenia	1,690	310

The effects of privatization on wage restraint have been more important than government wage policies. Most of the seven countries had a policy of limiting wage increases. For example, the Czech Republic, Hungary, and Poland had each implemented an excess wage tax at some point in the period 1991-1994. By 1995, all countries had market-determined wages. Even though government-led wage restraint applied primarily (or exclusively) to state-owned firms, wage growth in the state sector was higher than in the private sector in both Hungary and Poland. Bulgaria and the Slovak Republic pursued more vigorous wage restraint in the state sector, but real wages still outstripped productivity in contrast to the private sector.

A policy of limiting wages to encourage investment does not mean than wages must be constant. What matters is that they be held to a level below labor productivity. If labor productivity is increasing, wages can increase without impairing operating cash flow as long as they do not increase faster than labor productivity.

Financial restructuring

In addition to operational restructuring, many firms in the region need financial restructuring. These are firms that cannot service all of their outstanding debts; they are technically bankrupt or insolvent. It is important to determine when and how this financial restructuring should take place.

There are close links between operational and financial restructuring. One link is that rapid operational restructuring will improve the cash flow of a firm and reduce the need for financial restructuring. The opposing link is that financial restructuring may discourage operational restructuring depending on the circumstances.

The number of over-indebted firms in the region is large but declining. We define firms as being over-indebted if they do not have adequate cash flow to service all of their debt. Using the profit and loss categories shown in Table 1, these are the firms in categories C, D, and E. Figure 7 shows that the proportion of such firms in 1995 ranges from a high of more than 60 percent in Romania to a low of 6 percent in the Czech Republic.[17]

Financial restructuring of a firm can take a number of forms. First, if the firm can restructure its operations to achieve a positive operating cash flow, then the firm should continue in operation even though it may not be able to service all of its outstanding debts. In most cases, the lenders should

[17] This measure, however, can overestimate the financial difficulties of a firm in periods of high inflation. During high inflation, interest rates must increase to compensate the lender for the decline in value of the loan. The high interest payment is partly a repayment of the loan principal. In effect, high interest rates force firms to rapidly repay a sizable proportion of their outstanding loans in addition to the interest on the loans. Thus it is possible, for example, that the financial situation of Bulgarian and Romanian firms is not as bad as portrayed in Figure 7.

Government wage policies have been less successful than privatization.

Retained earnings and investment are higher in privatized firms.

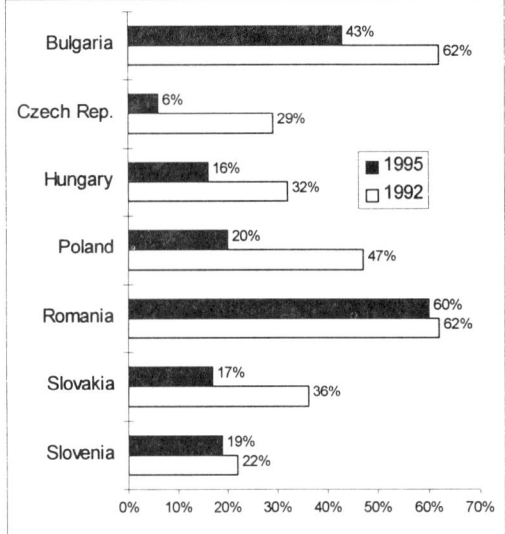

Figure 7: Proportion of industrial firms unable to service their debt
(weighted by employment)

Financial restructuring is usually done through voluntary negotiations.

The proportion of over-indebted firms is highest in Bulgaria and Romania.

agree to forgive (write off) some debts in exchange for this restructuring of the firm's operations. Second, if the firm has little chance of achieving a positive operating cash flow, the only alternative is liquidation: The firm ceases to operate, employees are laid off, and its assets are sold to pay at least some of its debts.

Although a well functioning bankruptcy system is essential, most financial restructuring of firms do not occur through the formal bankruptcy system. In Western countries, a high percentage of financial restructurings occur through voluntary negotiations between lenders and the firm. Only if the firm must be liquidated is it essential for a bankruptcy court to supervise the sale of assets and distribute the proceeds to creditors.

What actions, if any, should governments in the region take to encourage financial restructuring of over-indebted firms? In Western countries, most financial restructuring takes place through negotiations between private lenders (mostly banks) and private firms. However, in transition economies, most of the banks and many firms are still state-owned.

On the one hand, delay in financial restructuring may hinder operational restructuring. An over-indebted firm that could become profitable may not be able to borrow funds to pay for working capital, mod-

ernization, or expansion. This inability to borrow money is a common complaint of firms in the region. On the other hand, if the banks are not qualified to undertake these negotiations, there is a substantial risk that loans may be restructured or forgiven when, in fact, the firm could repay them. Also, by not reducing the firm's debt burden it may have a greater incentive to find ways to restructure its operations and improve cash flow.

Even worse, if a bank forgives part of its loans, a loss-making firm may be able to borrow additional funds that it cannot repay, which leads to even more bad loans held by the banks.[18] Large scale debt forgiveness could lead to relaxing the financial discipline on firms (hard budget constraint) that has finally been achieved in most countries of the region.

It should also be pointed out that firms in Western countries rely mostly on internal cash flow (retained earnings) to finance working capital or new investments rather than bank loans (see Table 10). In contrast, firms in the former socialist economies relied heavily on loans from state-owned banks and they now complain when this level of financing is no longer possible. Firms in the region, like their Western counterparts, must learn to finance their investments through increasing their own cash flow.

Table 10: Sources of net corporate financing in developed economies, 1970-89

(percent)	Germany	Japan	UK	US
Internal	81	69	97	91
Bank	11	31	20	16
Bonds	-1	5	4	17
Shares	1	4	-10	-9
Trade credit	-2	-8	-1	-4
Other	10	0	-8	-13

Early in the transition process, the level of firm indebtedness varied considerably from country to country due in part to the often ad-hoc nature of allocating invest-

---

[18] See Kotzeva and Perotti (1996) for a survey of Bulgarian firms that show such behavior.

ments under central planning. The ratio of bank debt to sales (see Figure 8) for the industrial firms in our sample was high in the two countries in which firms have restructured the least (Bulgaria and Romania) and high in the two countries with significant restructuring (Czech and Slovak Republics). This suggests that a high level of indebtedness does not necessarily discourage restructuring.

The econometric analysis at the firm level supports this view. We tested whether a high level of initial indebtedness relative to sales revenue hindered or encouraged operational restructuring. The evidence suggests that a high level of initial indebtedness either has no effect or actually encourages operational restructuring; i.e., the coefficients for indebtedness in the regression equation were either insignificant or positive.

This conclusion is supported by the case studies in the Slovak Republic. Most of these firms were highly indebted and thus had difficulty borrowing additional funds from the large Slovak state-owned banks. In many cases, they found alternative sources of finance, most importantly, their own internal cash flow. They had to undertake some restructuring to improve their cash flow, which was then used to finance further restructuring. In addition to internal cash flow, these firms were able to obtain some outside financing from customers, from foreign and domestic private banks, and through new joint venture arrangements that were not burdened with past debts.

On balance, special government policies to encourage the financial restructuring of firms may not be necessary. Financial restructuring can wait until after banks have been privatized and have developed the necessary negotiating skills and incentives. These banks have little to lose by not forgiving debt and much to gain if the firms can restructure, become more profitable, and repay more of their debt. A government sponsored program to encourage banks to forgive firm debt may actually slow down restructuring because it would weaken financial discipline.

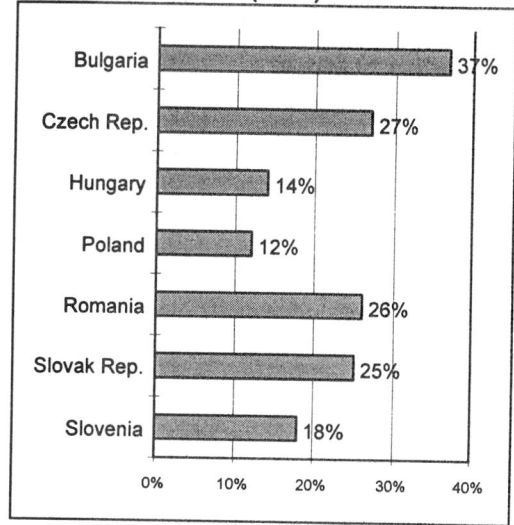

Figure 8: Ratio of total bank debt to sales for industrial firms (1992)

Bulgaria — 37%
Czech Rep. — 27%
Hungary — 14%
Poland — 12%
Romania — 26%
Slovak Rep. — 25%
Slovenia — 18%

Forgiving debt may discourage operational restructuring.

Negotiated financial restructurings, however, do not eliminate the need for a well functioning bankruptcy system to deal with those firms that must be liquidated. [19] Also banks may need to use the threat of swift bankruptcy and liquidation in order to force reluctant firms to undertake a negotiated financial restructuring. A good Commercial Code is also necessary.

Impact on bank restructuring

Although restructuring of firms is the primary subject of this paper, countries of the region also have to develop policies for the privatization, restructuring, and recapitalization of the former state-owned banks. Even with good progress in enterprise restructuring, many banks may end up burdened with loans made to firms unable to service those loans, i.e., pay interest or repay the principal when due. Consequently, some banks may not be able to repay their depositors and other liabilities.

If the government adopts policies that encourage restructuring, firms will be able to repay more of their bank loans. This will reduce the need to recapitalize the banking system and the consequent burden on tax payers. Enterprise restructuring is thus necessary to improve the health of the banking

In western countries, internal cash flow is the largest source of finance.

---

[19] See Gray et al. (1996) for a study of the Hungarian experience.

system. Nevertheless, some recapitalization may be needed eventually for some banks.

Another difficulty is how to predict the future profitability of firms. As the analysis above of restructuring shows, the profitability of firms in the region is changing much more rapidly (and randomly) than in mature market economies and so is their ability to service their debts.

To illustrate this point, we measure the ability of firms to service their debts. Our measure is based on their operating cash flow after paying wages and the cost of inputs. This cash-flow can be used to service at least part of the firm's debt.

For a specific year, we calculated the present discounted value of this cash flow assuming that it grows at a real rate of 4 percent per year thereafter.[20] The real discount rate used is 9 percent. This is an estimate of the real lending rate charged by banks in the region.[21] We call this discounted value the Debt Repayment Capacity for each firm. If it is less than the outstanding liabilities of the firm (bank loans, tax arrears, accounts payable less accounts receivable, etc.), the firm cannot repay all of its liabilities unless it restructures so as to improve its operating cash flow. We refer to this shortfall as the Uncollectable Liabilities for each firm.

Once the Uncollectable Liabilities of each firm is calculated, we sum over all firms and divide by the aggregate Total Liabilities. We refer to this ratio as the Aggregate Bad Loan Ratio. Although bank loans only make up a part of the total liabilities of a firm, we assume that all liabilities are paid off proportionally and bank loans do not receive a priority.

The Bad Loan Ratio had declined substantially by 1995 for most countries (Figure 9). In the Czech Republic, it decreased from

High level of indebtedness does not discourage restructuring.

Conventional measures of bad loans held by banks are unreliable in transition economies.

[20] In contrast to the estimated number of firms unable to service their debts in Figure 7, this estimate of the proportion of bad loans is not affected by inflation because an estimate of real cash flow is used.

[21] This is a simple average of the real bank lending rate in five countries (based on the producer price index) as estimated in Borish et al. (1996), Table 14, p. 35.

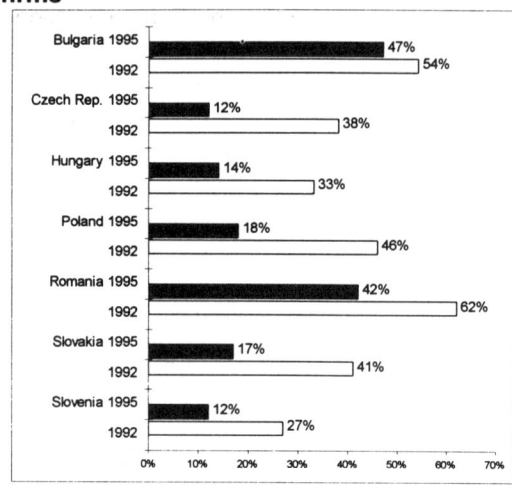

Figure 9: Bad loan ratio for industrial firms

38 percent in 1992 to 12 percent in 1995. In contrast, the Bad Loan Ratio started higher in Bulgaria and has only declined slightly.

Although based on reasonable assumptions, our estimate of the Bad Loan Ratio for 1992 is high because operating cash flow has grown faster than our assumption of 4 percent per year. Similarly, our estimate for 1995 is too high because firms in the region continue their rapid pace of restructuring. Conventional methods for estimating the bad loans of banks fail to recognize the rapid rate of restructuring in some countries and they overestimate the financial difficulty of banks and the cost of their recapitalization.

One inference from this analysis of bad loans is that governments should not rush to recapitalize banks because it is almost impossible to determine the true extent of their bad loans while restructuring is ongoing. Thus banks may receive an excessive recapitalization. Furthermore, recapitalization of banks will increase their ability to lend to firms. Firms in the region must learn to rely more on their own internal cash flow and less on bank loans. If recapitalization is done prior to the privatization of the banks, improvement in their lending skills, and privatization of enterprises, there is the risk of additional bad lending decisions, relaxed financial discipline for firms, and slower restructuring.

Sometimes bank recapitalization is combined with forgiving or writing off the bad loans to firms. However, we find little evidence that a high debt burden hinders restructuring.

If it does prove necessary to recapitalize the banks, this should be done as part of the privatization process. Only then can the government be certain that the banks will use these additional resources to encourage restructuring rather than to incur more bad loans that may require further recapitalization. The private banks can then begin to negotiate a financial restructuring of over-indebted firms. Again, delay in recapitalizing the banks or financially restructuring over-indebted firms is not likely to slow down the pace of operational restructuring.

Conclusions

One of the most important policy questions in the transition economies is what can governments do to speed up the restructuring of firms and thus hasten the transition to a mature market economy. The data that we have collected on the industrial firms in seven countries of the region as well as case studies provide some answers.

First, fast privatization is instrumental in encouraging restructuring. Less important is the method of privatization. Although case-by-case privatization might result in more foreign ownership, investment, and technical assistance, our case studies of Slovak firms suggest that this is not necessary for rapid restructuring. This is fortunate because such assistance is likely to be available for only a few firms even in those countries that emphasize case-by-case privatization. In most countries, firms were primarily sold to domestic investors (often managers and workers) rather than foreign investors.

What is needed instead is concentrated ownership. Mass privatization in the Czech and Slovak Republics resulted in a much more concentrated ownership structure than was originally predicted. Control of these firms by large strategic owners (including bank sponsored investment funds) also encouraged restructuring.

Second, we show that restraining wage increases to a level below increases in labor productivity allows for more restructuring. This increases the operating cash flow of firms, which can then be used to invest in modernization and expansion. As in mature market economies, most of the capital for new investment must come from the internal cash flow of the firm.

Third, policies that increase bank lending to firms (for example, recapitalizing the banks) or that forgive debts of firms may do more harm than good. The empirical analysis shows that was in the early years of transition, additional bank lending was most often associated with a decline in subsequent firm productivity. This suggests that increasing bank lending to firms or forgiving their debts tend to reduce financial discipline and thus the incentives for restructuring. Only when banking systems are sufficiently reformed and market-based do we observe a positive effect of increased bank lending on restructuring.

Fourth, it may be best to delay bank recapitalization. One important benefit of rapid restructuring is the increase in the ability of firms to repay their bank loans and other liabilities. This reduces the need for the government to recapitalize the banks in order to protect depositors. The safest course of action is to recapitalize the banks only as part of their privatization and to encourage them to negotiate the financial restructuring of firms including debt forgiveness only after they are privatized.

Rapid restructuring of firms will help the banks.

Bad loans have declined in most of the countries studied.

References

Barbone, Luca, Domenico Marchetti, and Stefano Paternostro 1996. Structural adjustment and ownership transformation: Poland's industrial performance in the early 1990s. World Bank Mimeo.

Borish, Michael S., Wei Ding, and Michel Noel. 1996. On the road to EU accession: financial sector development in Central Europe, World Bank. Discussion paper 345.

Carlin, Wendy, John Van Reenen, and Toby Wolfe. 1995. Enterprise restructuring in early transition: Case study evidence from Central and Eastern Europe". Economics of Transition, 3: 427-458.

Claessens, Stijn. 1997. Corporate Governance in the Czech Republic. Journal of Finance. (forthcoming)

Claessens, Stijn, Simeon Djankov and Gerhard Pohl. 1997a. Ownership and corporate governance: evidence from the Czech Republic. World Bank. Working paper 1737.

Claessens, Stijn, Simeon Djankov and Gerhard Pohl. 1997b. Determinants of restructuring of industrial firms in seven European transition economies. World Bank Mimeo.

Claessens, Stijn and R. Kyle Peters. 1997. Firm performance and soft budget constraints: the case of Bulgaria. *Economics of Transition.* (forthcoming)

Coffee, John. 1995. Corporate governance in Central Europe and Russia: institutional investors in transitional economies -- lesson from the Czech experience. World Bank Policy research paper 1450.

Djankov, Simeon and Bernard Hoekman. 1997a. Trade reorientation and post-reform productivity growth in Bulgarian firms *Journal of Policy Reform* (forthcoming)

Djankov, Simeon and Bernard Hoekman. 1997b. Avenues of technology transfer: foreign linkages and productivity change in the Czech Republic. World Bank Mimeo.

Djankov, Simeon and Gerhard Pohl. 1997a. Restructuring of large firms in The Slovak Republic. World Bank Working paper 1758.

Djankov, Simeon and Gerhard Pohl. 1997b. Does privatization matter? Evidence from Poland. World Bank Mimeo.

Gray, Cheryl, Sabine Schlorke, and Miklos Szanyi. 1996. Hungary's bankruptcy experience, 1992-93. *World Bank Economic Review.* 10:425-450.

Kotzeva, Mariana and Enrico Perotti. 1996. Rational creation of financial arrears: evidence from Bulgarian state managers. University of Amsterdam. Mimeo.

OECD 1996 *Trends and Policies in Privatization*, vol. III, no. 1.

Pohl, Gerhard, Simeon Djankov and Robert Anderson. 1996. Restructuring of large industrial firms in Central and Eastern Europe: an empirical analysis. World Bank Technical Paper 332.

Shleifer, Andrei and Robert Vishny. 1994. "Politicians and Firms," *Quarterly Journal of Economics*, 46: 995-1025.

Trend. 1996 Top 100 Slovak companies. Bratislava. December: p.11.

Table A1

We start with a standard neo-classical production function

$$Y_{it} = T_{it}[L_{it}^{s_{Li}} \ M_{it}^{s_{Mi}} \ K_{it}^{s_{Ki}}]^{\gamma_i}$$

where s_L, s_K and s_M are the shares of labor, capital and material inputs' expenditures in total expenditure for firm i and the T term equals total factor productivity change. To avoid imposing cost minimization, we estimate the marginal product of each input as follows:

$$\Delta y_{it} = \hat{\alpha}_i + \beta_{1s}\Delta l_{it} + \beta_{2s}\Delta m_{it} + \beta_{3s}\Delta k_{it} + \hat{\varepsilon}_{it}$$

where $y_{i,t} = \ln Y_{i,t} - \ln Y_{i,t-1}$ and similarly for $l_{i,t}$, $m_{i,t}$, and $k_{i,t}$. All β's are estimated over each industry (sector) s. The reported book value of fixed assets may be inaccurate and is unlikely to provide a good measure of the flow of capital services. Energy consumption is therefore used as a proxy for capital utilization. This correction has a number of desirable properties and is particularly attractive in the transition context because it is a flow measure that does not depend on fixed assets. Total factor productivity ($\Delta \hat{t}_{i,t}$) growth is then calculated as the sum of the residual and the firm-specific intercept.

$$\Delta \hat{t}_{it} = \hat{\alpha}_i + \hat{\varepsilon}_{it}$$

To properly control for other firm-specific factors, we augment the estimation as follows

$$\Delta y_{it} = \hat{\alpha}_i + \beta_{1s}\Delta l_{it} + \beta_{2s}\Delta m_{it} + \beta_{3s}\Delta k_{it} + \beta_4 \text{Size}_i +$$

$$+ \beta_5 \text{Privatization}_{i,t} + \beta_6 \text{Bank Financing}_{i,t} + \beta_7 T_{94} + \beta_8 T_{95} + \hat{\varepsilon}_{it}$$

Firm-specific variables:

Output - index of total quantity of goods sold defined as the value of sales deflated by the sector-specific producer price index in local currency.

Labor inputs - average number of workers adjusted for the average number of hours worked.

Material inputs - index of total material usage defined as the value of material inputs deflated by the sector-specific input price index in local currency.

Energy inputs - index of total energy usage defined as the value of energy inputs deflated by the aggregate energy price index in local currency.

Size - we rank all firms in a given sector by employment in the base year (1992) and then divide them into quartiles. We use dummies for each quartile. This specification proxies for market power *within* each sector.

Privatization - we divide all firms into cohorts depending on the number of years since their privatization. A separate dummy is used for each cohort.

Bank financing - change in bank financing in the preceding year.

Time - dummy variables for each year.

Table A2

Firm-specific variables:

Tobin's Q - the sum of market valuation plus total debt outstanding over the firm's replacement value (net fixed assets plus inventory).

Profitability - gross (operating) profit over net fixed assets plus inventory.

Leverage - ratio of assets to equity.

Dummy for first wave - 1 if the firm participated in the first wave of privatization, 0 otherwise.

Concentration - sum of shares of the top five investors, each raised to the second power.

Ownership - for each category (bank-sponsored investment funds, local strategic investors, etc.) the cumulative share of ownership in each firm.

Table A1: Results on privatization and financial discipline
(Dependent variable: Real Output Growth, panel regressions, random effects model)

Country	Bulgaria	Czech Rep.	Hungary	Poland	Romania	Slovak Rep.	Slovenia	All firms
Constant	-0.007	-0.037	-0.302*	-0.029	-0.167*	-0.033*	0.041*	0.055*
	(0.758)	(7.341)	(6.258)	(0.612)	(7.584)	(4.235)	(3.086)	(2.128)
Size Dummies included	Yes	Yes	Yes	Yes	Yes	Yes	Yes	Yes
Sector-specific production function included	Yes	Yes	Yes	Yes	Yes	Yes	Yes	Yes
Country x Time Dummies included								Yes
Dummy 1994	-0.107*	0.022*	0.035*	0.009*	-0.054*	0.057*	-0.123*	
	(9.691)	(2.722)	(7.129)	(1.989)	(4.537)	(6.354)	(5.003)	
Dummy 1995	0.275	-0.021	0.031*	0.017*	0.182*	0.045*	-0.058*	
	(0.296)	(1.328)	(5.668)	(3.754)	(8.029)	(5.162)	(3.258)	
Privatization Time Dummies								
1st Year	-0.033	0.063*	0.021*	0.011	-0.103*	0.044*	-0.008	0.029*
	(0.825)	(6.308)	(2.462)	(0.176)	(3.798)	(7.092)	(0.325)	(6.238)
2nd Year	0.152*	0.048*	0.039*	0.056*	0.086*	0.058*	0.079*	0.059*
	(4.245)	(7.048)	(5.207)	(9.924)	(3.126)	(4.251)	(6.945)	(9.985)
3rd Year	0.109*	0.025*	0.021*	0.054*	0.077*	0.062*	0.068*	0.054*
	(3.448)	(2.423)	(2.815)	(7.486)	(2.668)	(3.641)	(7.782)	(8.759)
Bank Financing 1993	-0.011	-0.023*	0.125*	-0.043*	-0.011	-0.018	-0.011	-0.004
	(0.827)	(2.568)	(9.537)	(6.745)	(0.839)	(0.285)	(0.329)	(0.896)
Bank Financing 1994	-0.010	0.008	0.139*	0.012**	-0.055*	0.010	0.009	0.008
	(1.285)	(0.135)	(9.892)	(1.768)	(3.621)	(0.118)	(0.542)	(1.038)
Bank Financing 1995	-0.028	0.018*	0.116*	0.015	-0.037*	0.021*	0.021**	0.013*
	(0.987)	(3.048)	(9.976)	(1.095)	(2.335)	(3.285)	(1.857)	(1.978)
Number of firms	828	706	1044	1066	1064	883	763	6354
Sample Size	2484	2118	3132	3198	3192	2649	2289	19062
Adjusted R^2	0.682	0.907	0.839	0.769	0.629	0.672	0.826	0.798

The estimates are heteroskedasticity consistent. t-Statistics shown in parentheses.

** Significant at the 90 percent level.

* Significant at the 95 percent level.

Table A2: Effect of ownership concentration in the Czech Republic
(Dependent Variables: Tobin's Q, Profitability, panel regression, random effects model)

Dependent variable	Regression I		Regression II		Regression III	
	Tobin's Q	Profit	Tobin's Q	Profit	Tobin's Q	Profit
Leverage	0.061 (13.462)*	-0.005 (4.618)*	0.059 (13.402)*	-0.005 (4.457)*	0.059 (13.432)*	-0.005 (4.459)*
Dummy for First Wave	0.120 (6.178)*	0.003 (0.306)	0.053 (2.415)*	0.006 (1.251)	0.051 (2.285)*	0.008 (1.192)
Concentration (Herfindahl Index)	0.217 (2.185)*	0.014 (0.648)	0.041 (0.116)	-0.061 (1.937)*	0.011 (0.142)	-0.095 (1.952)*
By Ownership: Bank Sponsored IPFs			0.398 (4.415)*	0.028 (1.415)	0.303 (3.305)*	0.018 (0.415)
Non-Bank Sponsored IPFs			0.068 (0.679)	0.011 (0.452)	0.068 (0.705)	0.011 (0.468)
National Property Fund			0.311 (1.891)**	0.024 (0.742)	0.312 (1.598)	0.022 (0.741)
Local Strategic Investors			-0.215 (1.574)	0.059 (1.639)	-0.215 (1.568)	0.053 (1.642)**
Foreign Strategic Investors			-0.048 (0.289)	0.118 (2.807)*	-0.033 (0.204)	0.122 (2.845)*
Conflict-of-interest Dummy					0.123 (4.065)*	0.0138 (1.686)**
Sector Dummies	Yes	Yes	Yes	Yes	Yes	Yes
Year Dummies	Yes	Yes	Yes	Yes	Yes	Yes
Number of firms	706	706	706	706	706	706
Sample Size	2824	2824	2824	2824	2824	2824
R^2	0.182	0.079	0.209	0.103	0.216	0.104

The estimates are heteroskedasticity consistent. t-Statistics shown in parentheses.

** Significant at the 90 percent level.

* Significant at the 95 percent level.

Table A3: Profit/loss categories for Bulgarian firms in 1995

	All Firms	Category A	Category B	Category C	Category D	Category E
Number of Firms	828	351	117	124	191	45
Employment	314,042	140,168	41,963	52,146	68,772	10,993
Employment %	100.00	44.63	13.36	16.60	21.90	3.50
Loans outstanding %	100.00	32.11	10.25	18.52	26.58	12.54
Sales revenue (bil. leva)	277,610	169,494	30,433	37,627	31,911	8,143
(% of Revenue)						
Sales revenue	100.00%	100.00%	100.00%	100.00%	100.00%	100.00%
minus cost of materials and energy	74.19%	71.90%	75.14%	68.48%	82.16%	113.49%
= Operating margin	25.81%	28.10%	24.86%	31.52%	17.84%	-13.49%
minus wages and wage taxes	15.41%	13.18%	17.67%	15.51%	24.75%	16.26%
= Operating cash flow	10.40%	14.92%	7.19%	16.02%	-6.92%	-29.75%
minus net financial charges	9.32%	3.49%	4.36%	26.39%	24.21%	11.81%
= Cash flow after debt service	1.08%	11.42%	2.83%	-10.38%	-31.12%	-41.56%
minus depreciation	3.14%	2.68%	4.90%	2.39%	4.10%	5.73%
= Net income before tax	-2.06%	8.74%	-2.07%	-12.77%	-35.22%	-47.29%
minus income tax	2.24%	3.50%	0.52%	0.15%	0.07%	0.55%
= Net income after tax	-4.30%	5.24%	-2.59%	-12.92%	-35.29%	-47.83%

Table A4: Profit/loss categories for Czech firms in 1995

	All Firms	Category A	Category B	Category C	Category D	Category E
Number of Firms	706	509	124	49	15	9
Employment	829,312	609,710	155,827	49,924	8,459	5,392
Employment %	100.00	73.52	18.79	6.02	1.02	0.65
Loans outstanding %	100.00	66.20	16.57	15.92	0.11	1.21
Sales revenue (mil. kroni)	568,307	463,680	77,731	22,350	2,951	1,593
(% of Revenue)						
Sales revenue	100.00%	100.00%	100.00%	100.00%	100.00%	100.00%
minus cost of materials and energy	69.61%	69.39%	68.52%	77.91%	68.83%	101.27%
= Operating margin	30.39%	30.61%	31.48%	22.09%	31.17%	-1.27%
minus wages and wage taxes	14.19%	12.87%	21.17%	16.91%	34.33%	9.62%
= Operating cash flow	16.20%	17.74%	10.31%	5.18%	-3.16%	-10.99%
minus net financial charges	3.40%	2.63%	4.79%	14.44%	5.93%	4.38%
= Cash flow after debt service	12.80%	15.11%	5.52%	-9.26%	-9.09%	-15.37%
minus depreciation	5.37%	5.02%	7.13%	6.50%	8.85%	4.22%
= Net income before tax	7.43%	10.09%	-1.61%	-15.76%	-17.94%	-19.59%
minus income tax	3.21%	3.91%	-0.01%	0.00%	0.00%	0.00%
= Net income after tax	4.22%	6.18%	-1.60%	-15.76%	-17.94%	-19.59%

Table A5: Profit/loss categories for Hungarian firms in 1995

	All Firms	Category A	Category B	Category C	Category D	Category E
Number of Firms	1,044	678	132	78	114	42
Employment	428,645	299,408	60,567	26,619	41,150	901
Employment %	100.00	69.85	14.13	6.21	8.96	0.85
Loans outstanding %	100.00	74.52	16.75	3.12	4.27	1.34
Sales revenue (mil. forints)	2,072,311	1,550,089	325,353	122,059	50,223	24,587
(% of Revenue)						
Sales revenue	100.00%	100.00%	100.00%	100.00%	100.00%	100.00%
minus cost of materials and energy	71.41%	69.22%	70.82%	75.42%	84.25%	103.34%
= Operating margin	28.59%	30.78%	29.18%	24.58%	15.75%	-3.34%
minus wages and wage taxes	14.42%	13.24%	16.35%	18.24%	19.87%	16.32%
= Operating cash flow	14.17%	17.54%	12.83%	6.34%	-4.12%	-19.66%
minus net financial charges	6.69%	5.42%	8.53%	11.28%	11.16%	9.87%
= Cash flow after debt service	7.48%	12.12%	4.30%	- 4.94%	-15.28%	-29.53%
minus depreciation	5.21%	6.23%	5.87%	6.98%	4.48%	5.64%
= Net income before tax	2.27%	5.89%	-1.57%	-11.92%	-19.76%	-35.17%
minus income tax	1.03%	3.24%	1.24%	0.00%	0.00%	0.00%
= Net income after tax	1.24%	2.65%	-2.81%	-11.92%	-19.76%	-35.17%

Table A6: Profit/loss categories for Romanian firms in 1995

	All Firms	Category A	Category B	Category C	Category D	Category E
Number of Firms	1092	277	137	104	447	127
Employment	2,121,102	503,220	338,319	192,914	854,550	232,099
Employment %	100.00	23.72	15.95	9.09	40.29	10.94
Loans outstanding %	100.00	12.54	9.98	11.47	52.35	13.66
Sales revenue (bil. lei)	46,013	12,442	10,396	7,937	10,385	4,851
(% of Revenue)						
Sales revenue	100.00%	100.00%	100.00%	100.00%	100.00%	100.00%
minus cost of materials and energy	80.73%	68.05%	73.39%	82.49%	78.36%	131.18%
= Operating margin	19.27%	31.95%	26.61%	17.51%	21.64%	-31.18%
minus wages and wage taxes	24.42%	20.02%	21.37%	12.63%	42.83%	22.16%
= Operating cash flow	-5.15%	11.93%	5.24%	4.88%	-21.19%	-53.35%
minus net financial charges	3.81%	0.58%	2.00%	9.08%	4.04%	6.88%
= Cash flow after debt service	-8.97%	11.35%	3.24%	-4.20%	-25.22%	-60.22%
minus depreciation	5.65%	5.61%	6.93%	4.60%	6.22%	3.53%
= Net income before tax	-14.62%	5.74%	-3.70%	-8.80%	-31.44%	-63.75%
minus income tax	1.53%	3.55%	0.68%	0.69%	0.93%	0.84%
= Net income after tax	-16.15%	2.19%	-4.38%	-9.48%	-32.37%	-64.59%

Table A7: Profit/loss categories for Slovak firms in 1995

	All Firms	Category A	Category B	Category C	Category D	Category E
Number of Firms	905	319	250	80	241	15
Employment	578,737	322,241	157,648	41,958	53,301	3,589
Employment %	100.00	55.68	27.24	7.25	9.21	0.42
Loans outstanding %	100.00	51.09	18.87	12.01	16.60	1.44
Sales revenue (mil. kroni)	339,328	247,985	49,900	17,339	23,123	979
(% of Revenue)						
Sales revenue	100.00%	100.00%	100.00%	100.00%	100.00%	100.00%
minus cost of materials and energy	67.58%	67.45%	61.40%	74.82%	74.85%	115.59%
= Operating margin	32.42%	32.55%	38.60%	25.18%	25.15%	-15.59%
minus wages and wage taxes	16.87%	12.33%	28.55%	22.32%	35.95%	26.67%
= Operating cash flow	15.55%	20.22%	10.05%	2.86%	-10.80%	-42.27%
minus net financial charges	1.02%	-0.68%	3.49%	8.15%	7.77%	20.94%
= Cash flow after debt service	14.52%	20.90%	6.56%	-5.29%	-18.57%	-63.20%
minus depreciation	6.89%	5.63%	10.20%	7.96%	12.10%	16.29%
= Net income before tax	7.63%	15.27%	-3.64%	-13.25%	-30.67%	-79.50%
minus income tax	4.84%	6.50%	0.38%	0.31%	0.22%	0.36%
= Net income after tax	2.79%	8.77%	-4.02%	-13.56%	-30.89%	-79.85%

Table A8: Profit/loss categories for Slovenian firms in 1995

	All Firms	Category A	Category B	Category C	Category D	Category E
Number of Firms	727	508	86	70	52	11
Employment	219,959	141,636	37,173	19,805	17,263	4,082
Employment %	100.00	64.39	16.90	9.00	7.85	1.86
Loans outstanding %	100.00	68.93	18.25	7.85	4.21	0.76
Sales revenue (mil. tolars)	2,368,239	1,795,788	252,715	192,054	96,185	31,494
(% of Revenue)						
Sales revenue	100.00%	100.00%	100.00%	100.00%	100.00%	100.00%
minus cost of materials and energy	78.47%	77.77%	74.65%	80.83%	86.38%	110.44%
= Operating margin	21.53%	22.23%	25.35%	19.17%	13.62%	-10.44%
minus wages and wage taxes	12.17%	11.38%	15.79%	11.70%	18.58%	11.87%
= Operating cash flow	9.36%	10.86%	9.56%	7.47%	-4.96%	-22.31%
minus net financial charges	4.86%	3.46%	6.15%	12.38%	10.38%	11.49%
= Cash flow after debt service	4.50%	7.40%	3.41%	-4.91%	-15.34%	-33.80%
minus depreciation	4.49%	4.33%	6.62%	3.47%	3.82%	4.95%
= Net income before tax	0.01%	3.07%	-3.21%	-8.38%	-19.17%	-38.75%
minus income tax	0.32%	0.43%	0.00%	0.00%	0.00%	0.00%
= Net income after tax	-0.31%	2.64%	-3.21%	-8.38%	-19.17%	-38.75%

POHL, ANDERSON, CLAESSENS, DJANKOV

Distributors of World Bank Publications

Prices and credit terms vary from country to country. Consult your local distributor before placing an order.

ARGENTINA
Oficina del Libro Internacional
Av. Cordoba 1877
1120 Buenos Aires
Tel: (54 1) 815-8354
Fax: (54 1) 815-8156

AUSTRALIA, FIJI, PAPUA NEW GUINEA, SOLOMON ISLANDS, VANUATU, AND WESTERN SAMOA
D.A. Information Services
648 Whitehorse Road
Mitcham 3132
Victoria
Tel: (61) 3 9210 7777
Fax: (61) 3 9210 7788
E-mail: service@dadirect.com.au
URL: http://www.dadirect.com.au

AUSTRIA
Gerold and Co.
Weihburggasse 26
A-1011 Wien
Tel: (43 1) 512-47-31-0
Fax: (43 1) 512-47-31-29
URL: http://www.gerold.co/at.online

BANGLADESH
Micro Industries Development Assistance Society (MIDAS)
House 5, Road 16
Dhanmondi R/Area
Dhaka 1209
Tel: (880 2) 326427
Fax: (880 2) 811188

BELGIUM
Jean De Lannoy
Av. du Roi 202
1060 Brussels
Tel: (32 2) 538-5169
Fax: (32 2) 538-0841

BRAZIL
Publicacoes Tecnicas Internacionais Ltda.
Rua Peixoto Gomide, 209
01409 Sao Paulo, SP
Tel: (55 11) 259-6644
Fax: (55 11) 258-6990
E-mail: postmaster@pti.uol.br
URL: http://www.uol.br

CANADA
Renouf Publishing Co. Ltd.
5369 Canotek Road
Ottawa, Ontario K1J 9J3
Tel: (613) 745-2665
Fax: (613) 745-7660
E-mail: order.dept@renoufbooks.com
URL: http://www.renoufbooks.com

CHINA
China Financial & Economic Publishing House
8, Da Fo Si Dong Jie
Beijing
Tel: (86 10) 6333-8257
Fax: (86 10) 6401-7365

COLOMBIA
Infoenlace Ltda.
Carrera 6 No. 51-21
Apartado Aereo 34270
Santafé de Bogotá, D.C.
Tel: (57 1) 285-2798
Fax: (57 1) 285-2798

COTE D'IVOIRE
Center d'Edition et de Diffusion Africaines (CEDA)
04 B.P. 541
Abidjan 04
Tel: (225) 24 6510;24 6511
Fax: (225) 25 0567

CYPRUS
Center for Applied Research
Cyprus College
6, Diogenes Street, Engomi
P.O. Box 2006
Nicosia
Tel: (357 2) 44-1730
Fax: (357 2) 46-2051

CZECH REPUBLIC
National Information Center
prodejna, Konviktská 5
CS – 113 57 Prague 1
Tel: (42 2) 2422-9433
Fax: (42 2) 2422-1484
URL: http://www.nis.cz/

DENMARK
SamfundsLitteratur
Rosenoerns Allé 11
DK-1970 Frederiksberg C
Tel: (45 31) 351942
Fax: (45 31) 357822

EGYPT, ARAB REPUBLIC OF
Al Ahram Distribution Agency
Al Galaa Street
Cairo
Tel: (20 2) 578-6083
Fax: (20 2) 578-6833

The Middle East Observer
41, Sherif Street
Cairo
Tel: (20 2) 393-9732
Fax: (20 2) 393-9732

FINLAND
Akateeminen Kirjakauppa
P.O. Box 128
FIN-00101 Helsinki
Tel: (358 0) 121 4418
Fax: (358 0) 121-4435
E-mail: akatilaus@stockmann.fi
URL: http://www.akateeminen.com/

FRANCE
World Bank Publications
66, avenue d'Iéna
75116 Paris
Tel: (33 1) 40-69-30-56/57
Fax: (33 1) 40-69-30-68

GERMANY
UNO-Verlag
Poppelsdorfer Allee 55
53115 Bonn
Tel: (49 228) 212940
Fax: (49 228) 217492

GREECE
Papasotiriou S.A.
35, Stournara Str.
106 82 Athens
Tel: (30 1) 364-1826
Fax: (30 1) 364-8254

HAITI
Culture Diffusion
5, Rue Capois
C.P. 257
Port-au-Prince
Tel: (509 1) 3 9260

HONG KONG, MACAO
Asia 2000 Ltd.
Sales & Circulation Department
Seabird House, unit 1101-02
22-28 Wyndham Street, Central
Hong Kong
Tel: (852) 2530-1409
Fax: (852) 2526-1107
E-mail: sales@asia2000.com.hk
URL: http://www.asia2000.com.hk

INDIA
Allied Publishers Ltd.
751 Mount Road
Madras - 600 002
Tel: (91 44) 852-3938
Fax: (91 44) 852-0649

INDONESIA
Pt. Indira Limited
Jalan Borobudur 20
P.O. Box 181
Jakarta 10320
Tel: (62 21) 390-4290
Fax: (62 21) 421-4289

IRAN
Ketab Sara Co. Publishers
Khaled Eslamboli Ave.,
6th Street
Kusheh Delafrooz No. 8
P.O. Box 15745-733
Tehran
Tel: (98 21) 8717819; 8716104
Fax: (98 21) 8712479
E-mail: ketab-sara@neda.net.ir

Kowkab Publishers
P.O. Box 19575-511
Tehran
Tel: (98 21) 258-3723
Fax: (98 21) 258-3723

IRELAND
Government Supplies Agency
Oifig an tSoláthair
4-5 Harcourt Road
Dublin 2
Tel: (353 1) 661-3111
Fax: (353 1) 475-2670

ISRAEL
Yozmot Literature Ltd.
P.O. Box 56055
3 Yohanan Hasandlar Street
Tel Aviv 61560
Tel: (972 3) 5285-397
Fax: (972 3) 5285-397

R.O.Y. International
PO Box 13056
Tel Aviv 61130
Tel: (972 3) 5461423
Fax: (972 3) 5461442
E-mail: royil@netvision.net.il

Palestinian Authority/Middle East
Index Information Services
P.O.B. 19502 Jerusalem
Tel: (972 2) 6271219
Fax: (972 2) 6271634

ITALY
Licosa Commissionaria Sansoni SPA
Via Duca Di Calabria, 1/1
Casella Postale 552
50125 Firenze
Tel: (55) 645-415
Fax: (55) 641-257
E-mail: licosa@ftbcc.it
Url: http://www.ftbcc.it//licosa

JAMAICA
Ian Randle Publishers Ltd.
206 Old Hope Road
Kingston 6
Tel: 809-927-2085
Fax: 809-977-0243
E-mail: irpl@colis.com

JAPAN
Eastern Book Service
3-13 Hongo 3-chome, Bunkyo-ku
Tokyo 113
Tel: (81 3) 3818-0861
Fax: (81 3) 3818-0864
E-mail: orders@svt-ebs.co.jp
URL: http://www.bekkoame.or.jp/~svt-ebs

KENYA
Africa Book Service (E.A.) Ltd.
Quaran House, Mfangano Street
P.O. Box 45245
Nairobi
Tel: (254 2) 223 641
Fax: (254 2) 330 272

KOREA, REPUBLIC OF
Daejon Trading Co. Ltd.
P.O. Box 34, Youida
706 Seoun Bldg
44-6 Youido-Dong, Yeongchengo-Ku
Seoul
Tel: (82 2) 785-1631/4
Fax: (82 2) 784-0315

MALAYSIA
University of Malaya Cooperative Bookshop, Limited
P.O. Box 1127
Jalan Pantai Baru
59700 Kuala Lumpur
Tel: (60 3) 756-5000
Fax: (60 3) 755-4424

MEXICO
INFOTEC
Av. San Fernando No. 37
Col. Toriello Guerra
14050 Mexico, D.F.
Tel: (52 5) 624-2800
Fax: (52 5) 624-2822
E-mail: infotec@rtn.net.mx
URL: http://rtn.net.mx

NEPAL
Everest Media International Services (P) Ltd.
GPO Box 5443
Kathmandu
Tel: (977 1) 472 152
Fax: (977 1) 224 431

NETHERLANDS
De Lindeboom/InOr-Publikaties
P.O. Box 202
7480 AE Haaksbergen
Tel: (31 53) 574-0004
Fax: (31 53) 572-9296
E-mail: lindeboom@worldonline.nl
URL: http://www.worldonline.nl/-lindeboo

NEW ZEALAND
EBSCO NZ Ltd.
Private Mail Bag 99914
New Market
Auckland
Tel: (64 9) 524-8119
Fax: (64 9) 524-8067

NIGERIA
University Press Limited
Three Crowns Building Jericho
Private Mail Bag 5095
Ibadan
Tel: (234 22) 41-1356
Fax: (234 22) 41-2056

NORWAY
NIC Info A/S
Book Department
Postboks 6512 Etterstad
N-0606 Oslo
Tel: (47 22) 97-4500
Fax: (47 22) 97-4545

PAKISTAN
Mirza Book Agency
65, Shahrah-e-Quaid-e-Azam
Lahore 54000
Tel: (92 42) 735 3601
Fax: (92 42) 758 5283

Oxford University Press
5 Bangalore Town
Sharae Faisal
PO Box 13033
Karachi-75350
Tel: (92 21) 446307
Fax: (92 21) 4547640
E-mail: oup@oup.khi.erum.com.pk

Pak Book Corporation
Aziz Chambers 21
Queen's Road
Lahore
Tel: (92 42) 636 3222; 636 0885
Fax: (92 42) 636 2328

PERU
Editorial Desarrollo SA
Apartado 3824
Lima 1
Tel: (51 14) 285380
Fax: (51 14) 286628

PHILIPPINES
International Booksource Center Inc.
1127-A Antipolo St.
Barangay, Venezuela
Makati City
Tel: (63 2) 896 6501; 6505; 6507
Fax: (63 2) 896 1741

POLAND
International Publishing Service
Ul. Piekna 31/37
00-677 Warzawa
Tel: (48 2) 628-6089
Fax: (48 2) 621-7255
URL: http://www.ipscg.waw.pl/ips/export/

PORTUGAL
Livraria Portugal
Apartado 2681
Rua Do Carmo 70-74
1200 Lisbon
Tel: (1) 347-4982
Fax: (1) 347-0264

ROMANIA
Compani De Librari Bucuresti S.A.
Str. Lipscani no. 26, sector 3
Bucharest
Tel: (40 1) 613 9645
Fax: (40 1) 312 4000

RUSSIAN FEDERATION
Isdatelstvo <Ves Mir>
9a, Lolpachniy Pereulok
Moscow 101831
Tel: (7 095) 917 87 49
Fax: (7 095) 917 92 59

SINGAPORE, TAIWAN, MYANMAR, BRUNEI
Asahgate Publishing Asia Pacific Pte. Ltd.
41 Kallang Pudding Road #04-03
Golden Wheel Building
Singapore 349316
Tel: (65) 741-5166
Fax: (65) 742-9356
E-mail: ashgate@asianconnect.com

SLOVENIA
Gospodarski Vestnik Publishing Group
Dunajska cesta 5
1000 Ljubljana
Tel: (386 61) 133 83 47; 132 12 30
Fax: (386 61) 133 80 30
E-mail: belicd@gvestnik.si

SOUTH AFRICA, BOTSWANA
For single titles:
Oxford University Press Southern Africa
P.O. Box 1141
Cape Town 8000
Tel: (27 21) 45-7266
Fax: (27 21) 45-7265

For subscription orders:
International Subscription Service
P.O. Box 41095
Craighall
Johannesburg 2024
Tel: (27 11) 880-1448
Fax: (27 11) 880-6248
E-mail: iss@is.co.za

SPAIN
Mundi-Prensa Libros, S.A.
Castello 37
28001 Madrid
Tel: (34 1) 431-3399
Fax: (34 1) 575-3998
E-mail: libreria@mundiprensa.es
URL: http://www.mundiprensa.es/

Mundi-Prensa Barcelona
Consell de Cent, 391
08009 Barcelona
Tel: (34 3) 488-3492
Fax: (34 3) 487-7659
E-mail: barcelona@mundiprensa.es

SRI LANKA, THE MALDIVES
Lake House Bookshop
100, Sir Chittampalam Gardiner Mawatha
Colombo 2
Tel: (94 1) 32105
Fax: (94 1) 432104
E-mail: LHL@sri.lanka.net

SWEDEN
Wennergren-Williams AB
P. O. Box 1305
S-171 25 Solna
Tel: (46 8) 705-97-50
Fax: (46 8) 27-00-71
E-mail: mail@wwi.se

SWITZERLAND
Librarie Payot Service Institutionnel
Côtes-de-Montbenon 30
1002 Lausanne
Tel: (41 21) 341-3229
Fax: (41 21) 341-3235

ADECO Van Diermen EditionsTechniques
Ch. de Lacuez 41
CH1807 Blonay
Tel: (41 21) 943 2673
Fax: (41 21) 943 3605

TANZANIA
Oxford University Press
Maktaba Street
PO Box 5299
Dar es Salaam
Tel: (255 51) 29209
Fax: (255 51) 46822

THAILAND
Central Books Distribution
306 Silom Road
Bangkok 10500
Tel: (66 2) 235-5400
Fax: (66 2) 237-8321

TRINIDAD & TOBAGO, AND THE CARRIBEAN
Systematics Studies Unit
9 Watts Street
Curepe
Trinidad, West Indies
Tel: (809) 662-5654
Fax: (809) 662-5654
E-mail: tobe@trinidad.net

UGANDA
Gustro Ltd.
PO Box 9997, Madhvani Building
Plot 16/4 Jinja Rd.
Kampala
Tel: (256 41) 254 763
Fax: (256 41) 251 468

UNITED KINGDOM
Microinfo Ltd.
P.O. Box 3
Alton, Hampshire GU34 2PG
England
Tel: (44 1420) 86848
Fax: (44 1420) 89889
E-mail: wbank@ukminfo.demon.co.uk
URL: http://www.microinfo.co.uk

VENEZUELA
Tecni-Ciencia Libros, S.A.
Centro Cuidad Comercial Tamanco
Nivel C2
Caracas
Tel: (58 2) 959 5547; 5035; 0016
Fax: (58 2) 959 5636

ZAMBIA
University Bookshop, University of Zambia
Great East Road Campus
P.O. Box 32379
Lusaka
Tel: (260 1) 252 576
Fax: (260 1) 253 952

ZIMBABWE
Longman Zimbabwe (Pvt.)Ltd.
Tourle Road, Ardbennie
P.O. Box ST125
Southerton
Harare
Tel: (263 4) 6216617
Fax: (263 4) 621670

04/28/97